Landscape and Distance
Contemporary Poets from Virginia

Landscape and Distance

Contemporary Poets from Virginia

Margaret Gibson and Richard McCann, Editors

University Press of Virginia
Charlottesville

THE UNIVERSITY PRESS OF VIRGINIA
Copyright © 1975 by the Rector and Visitors
of the University of Virginia

First published 1975

Library of Congress Cataloging in Publication Data

Gibson, Margaret, comp.
    Landscape and distance.

    Poems.
    1. American poetry—Virginia. 2. American
poetry—20th century. I. McCann, Richard J.,
joint comp. II. Title. PS558.V5G5   811'.5'408
75-2350   ISBN 0-8139-0622-9

Printed in the United States of America

To the memory of Jean Farley

Foreword

As a northerner moving slowly but inexorably south, I find that it has taken me half my life to come only as far as Maryland. But from where I live now it is just a few miles, as the crow flies, to the Potomac River. Across that river lies Virginia, to me at least, the beginning of the real South.

I am learning to know Virginia gradually, as any reticent neighbor might. I have made forays over the bridge in my car; I have given workshops at some of its colleges and universities; and I have read quite a bit of the prose and poetry of Virginia writers.

Recently I visited Monticello for the first time. There, in a gift shop, among souvenir dish towels and ash trays I came across a facimile of the following passage from a letter written by Thomas Jefferson, possibly the most famous Virginian of all. He was explaining to his friend William Short why there never had been a poet north of the Alps. And in doing so he wrote: "A poet is as much a creature of climate as an orange or palm tree. What a bird the nightingale would be in the climate of America."

Nearly two hundred years later, and from a very different perspective, Victor Lange might have been concurring when he stated that "at a time when the purpose and forms of art tend to become ever more universal it is well to remember that works of the imagination always spring from the specific impulses of place and time."

Here then is a collection of poems by my neighboring Virginians, many of them written from just such impulses.

"After three months Virginia is still a frontier," says one of these poets, and in this book we are allowed to cross that frontier, to enter a landscape filled with milk cow farmers, fenced pastures, small public libraries, smallmouth bass, creeks, hoofs, and "sweet water falling over rock."

I do not mean to imply that these poems are in any way narrow or parochial or that they represent a particular school of writing or of criticism. They are not like the so-called New York School or the Black Mountain School. Nor can they be categorized the way Edmund Wilson, for example, categorized another group of southerners, the Tennessee poets of the Fugitive.

For there is a great range here. These poems move from the spare lyricism of Joseph Garrison's "Moonset" to the rich textures of Annie Dillard's "Feast Days," from the free, almost prosy structure of Alan Williamson's "A Progress of the Soul" to the formal sweetness of William Jay Smith's "Picture of Her Bones" and the virtuosity of Henry Taylor's "Burning a Horse."

In a poem about vision, a poem itself rooted firmly in a particular place, Dabney Stuart reminds us that the poet is dealing with "Not the aspect of a particular place / But only, reflected, his own face."

And so these poems, starting as they do in contemporary Virginia, carry us not only backwards into the past, to all the "Houses We've Lived In"; not only outward to Venice in fog, to the Caribbean; but to the many inner places, some of them dark indeed, that William Jay Smith's "monsters of the mind's making" can carry us.

In a special prose section the writers of this book have added some specific reflections on "Landscape and Distance," the theme that gives the book its title. These paragraphs, among other things, show clearly how nomadic we Americans have become since Jefferson's time. Some of the poets turn out to be native Virginians, some Virginians by adoption or necessity; some are only passing through. All of them reflect to some degree the feeling of movement in America, even when the poet is doing no more than watching geese flying by or trains passing.

Nevertheless, what gives this book its unity, its particular flavor, is that over and over again Virginia itself becomes a kind of native touchstone. "This field seems the center," as Jean Farley puts it.

In part of a long poem Annie Dillard writes:

> "Home," I say to the cabby,
> "home, driver, to Tinker Creek.
> It's in Virginia."
> And he says, "Sorry, honey,
> you can't get there from here."

Maybe not, but with this book you can at least get part of the way.

Linda Pastan
Potomac, Maryland

Acknowledgments

For permission to reprint poems that first appeared in various magazines and books, the authors, publisher, and editors wish to express their grateful acknowledgement to:

The University of North Carolina Press for "A World of Watchfulness," "The Night Horse," "Snow Blindness," and "Scroll," by Jean Farley and published in *Figure and Field*©1970 by University of North Carolina Press.

The *New Yorker* for "Spring Trains," ©1974 The New Yorker Magazine, Inc.; and to *Shenandoah* for "A Progress of the Soul," both by Alan Williamson.

George Braziller, Inc., for "Pause, in Flight" and "The Skipped Page" from *Welcome, Eumenides*, by Eleanor Ross Taylor, reprinted with the permission of the publisher, Copyright©1972 by Eleanor Ross Taylor.

Delacorte Press-Seymour Lawrence for "The Angry Man" and "A Picture of Her Bones," from *The Tin Can and Other Poems* by William Jay Smith, Copyright©1966 by William Jay Smith. Used with permission of Delacorte Press-Seymour Lawrence. And the *New York Times* for "Venice in Fog"© 1973 by the New York Times Company. Reprinted by permission.

The *Virginia Quarterly Review* for "Flight," by Amanda Bullins.

Shenandoah for "Reddish Knob: From the Firetower," by Joseph Garrison.

The University of North Carolina Press for "Alligator Night" and "Walking Home from the Raleigh Court Branch Public Library," by R. H. W. Dillard, published in *News of the Nile*, © 1971 and the Louisiana State University Press for "Rain" and "Limits," by R. H. W. Dillard, published in *After Borges*, © 1972.

The *New Republic* for "Entreaties," by Rudy Shackelford. Reprinted by permission of *The New Republic*,©1972 *The New Republic*, Inc.

Esquire for "Watching the Traveler," reprinted by permission of *Esquire Magazine*© 1973 by Esquire, Inc.; and *Shenandoah* for "You Ask Me How I'm Doing, I Tell You," both by Richard McCann.

Shenandoah for "What Got Through"; and *The American Poetry Review* for "To the Farmer of Milk Cows," both by Peter Fellowes.

Dabney Stuart for "Sticks and Stones," "Goshen Pass: Winter," and "Love Letter," from *A Particular Place*,©Dabney Stuart, 1969; and Louisiana State University Press for "Vision," by Dabney Stuart, from *The Other Hand*,©1974 by Dabney Stuart.

The Iowa Review for "Miracles," by James Everhard.

Shenandoah for "Baking at the Beach," by Kate Jennings.

The Ohio University Press for "The Lost Hunter in the Dismal Swamp" and "The Wives at Old Point Comfort," from *The Fisherman's Whore* ©1974 by David Jeddie Smith. "The Lost Hunter in the Dismal Swamp" appeared previously in the *Northwest Review*.

Winthrop Publishers, Inc., for "Lighthouse Keeper," by Gary Sange. Reprinted by permission of the author and of Winthrop Publishers, Inc., from *New Voices in American Poetry: An Anthology*. Edited by David Allen Evans©1973.

Shenandoah for "Houses We Lived In," by Bruce Guernsey.

The Golden Quill Press for "A Word to a Father, Dead," by John Alexander Allen, from *The Lean Divider*,©1968.

The University of Utah Press for "Burning a Horse," copyright©1970 by Henry Taylor, and "Riding a One-Eyed Horse," copyright©by Henry Taylor, reprinted from the book *An Afternoon of Pocket Billiards* by permission of the author and The University of Utah Press. "Burning a Horse" appeared previously in the *Southern Review* and in *Breakings* (Solo Press, 1971); "Riding a One-Eyed Horse" appeared previously in *Practical Horseman* and *Carolina Quarterly*.

The University of Missouri Press for "Feast Days," reprinted from *Tickets for a Prayer Wheel*, by Annie Dillard, by permission of the author and the University of Missouri Press. Copyright 1974 by Annie Dillard. And the *Atlantic Monthly* for a portion of "Feast Days" entitled "Feast Days: Christmas." Copyright©1973, by The Atlantic Monthly Company, Boston, Mass. Reprinted with permission.

Poetry for "Alternate Lives," by Anne Winters, copyright© May, 1973, by the Modern Poetry Association, reprinted by permission of the editor of *Poetry*.

Alfred A. Knopf for "Kinderscenen," "Loving 1," "Dream 2," and "The Bennett Springs Road." From *Adam's Dream*, by Julia Randall, Copyright©1966, 1967, 1968, 1969 by Julia Randall Sawyer. Reprinted by permission of Alfred A. Knopf, Inc; *The Red Clay Reader* for "Letter," by Julia Randall; and the University of North Carolina Press for "Science and Poetry: Three Comments," from *The Puritan Carpenter*, Copyright©1961, 1962, 1964, 1965 by Julia Randall Sawyer.

The editors wish to express their thanks to Walton Beacham for his invaluable assistance and advice.

Contents

Landscape and Distance
Contemporary Poets from Virginia

JEAN FARLEY

A World of Watchfulness

This quiet, briar-filled wire,
The ingrown fencing of a pasture
So simply left that from its center
The edge seems unreal as an outer coast,
Has no tautness.
Hanging by its vines
From loose barked, logy posts
Which lie against the sky like spires,
It is difficult to climb.

When from the strangeness of inner space
I watch the wind-struck weeds
Which dip toward the fence and, rooted, scatter,
Or the shadows of gulls
That on some brilliant wake
Bounce like leaves
While their gulls on wind wheel, freely, flatter;
When, half looking from under my brow,
I see a woman approach and chatter,
Forget herself in excited ease
And, shifting from her left to right leg, shorter,
Smile from a gently bobbing head—
This field seems the center
Of all I have watched, confused, not said.

The Night Horse

I awake an hour before dawn
And still she grazes there,
Slipped somewhere out of the field of sight
But ripping and chewing spring grass
Which grows longer now, gaining momentum:
After the first low hesitant start
It pours forth from the ground
Almost as fast as rain went in.
The horse grazes on the edge of attention;
Half between sleep and feigning sleep,
I dare not look too close or she will go.
Now that there are leaves the wind blows
Like a bear turning over from sleep—
Stirs and rustles and goes.
Silence then, the horse I cannot see
Grazing in the dark at the edge of the woods.
If I could go to her as simply
As the single night song of a bird
Reaches out of the woods—
Reach for her mane and be on her back—
The wind turns over, dawn begins
And the babble of many small birds.

Snow Blindness

The crust of this temperate portion of earth
Has swollen all day and all night
Two feet thicker with snow.
A cross section now would show
On layers of bedrock, marl, and clay
The minute umber graves of loam
Surmounted by sudden epethelial growth.
Round black boles of trees
Bristle at every angle
And birds therein live vividly on hope.

The freeze holds day after day;
Slowly the roads are cleared
And all the birds of this covered land
Seem to cluster there weakening,
Killed by cars, feeding on grit.
A blackbird in a coasting fall
Ends on his back in powdery snow
Under the stabbing beak of a mockingbird
Who will sing through all the moonlit nights
Of summer—if he lives.

Coming inside, gleaming with cold,
A film of snow upon my eyes,
I grope for a moment,
Reclaim the borders of my head,
Think it the easiest virtue I ever knew
To throw feed for gathering birds
On the bare dirt floor of an open shed—
That noted through summer ways
They may go hedgehopping, flying,
Singing, and finding about my house all day.

Awake in the night, I hear my brain stir,
Feeding on doubt behind my eyes:
How do you say that in a dazzling world
Of new snow, you move in the dark,
In the house, hands stretched out
To fend away a door opening the wrong way,
The corner of a table the size of a grave,
Steps, a fragile chair, any onrushing thing

Forgotten from the blueprint confronting your mind
So close it wraps you in
Closer than your own skin?

As though the poster in a comedy, slapped
On the face of bystander with miraculous glue,
Had melted without a trace through skin
To invisibly seal off the brain behind eyes.
What then, what do you do—
Hilarious figure—daubed, stumbling
With poster and insoluble glue?
Better to stop, affect an air
That it isn't there, or you aren't there,
Merge with a wall and think the thing through:

Though you are in a panic to be free
You cannot wake the sleeping house,
Cannot fight your way out.
Besides, what good would it do
To regain the world of light
Which, a little too loud and cheerful,
You have always blundered through?
Whatever the film that impedes your eyes,
Dark in light, light in dark,
Is one layer of the blinding skin you live inside.

Scroll

When low mild layers of earth-round wind
Unfurl the inner, lull the outer skin—
The trees of distant war, as in a dream,
Are very green, unpredictable of limb,
A little pressed for space, jostling
Triumphant as emblems
Above a march that will never start.
The fusillade which must sound there
Rolls back upon itself in air
And there in the grey green river valley
Which creases the other side of the world
Ten or a thousand soldiers hear
With a single ear
That peculiar snap which takes the quirk
From their curvature of time.
They are rolled up, fastened,
And set aside now, sadly
As an ancient Chinese river scroll:
None of their blood seeps to the spine.

ALAN WILLIAMSON

Spring Trains

In spring one notices the trains more,
in their unaging childhood:
the rust-red boxcars, the blue-black coal scuttles on wheels,
stopped a long time, then imperceptibly moving
through the new green lash
of the willows . . .

I think they will go by the windows of lonely peaked houses
where sómeone smudged and beautiful
draws one hair back over the seashell of her ear;
and I think they go to the night I once woke to,
dark peaks swinging from side to side of the sky,
and the rapids beneath shades paler than the snow,
while the Mormon evangelist wheezed in the next chair;
and sometimes I think they go to a secret mountain
in the center of West Virginia,
made of coal so black it is everywhere a mirror,
and you never know the moment of passing through.

A Progress of the Soul

In the beginning there are your limbs crossing simply
as the beams cross in the summer cottage ceiling
—pine-soap smell from the bath—

and there is a story, that goes as many ways
as the cobwebs in the corner. In it, the dead get married
as often as they baptized in Brigham Young's
Temple, and through the same medium, our pale bodies.
Before you have pubic hair you see the gown
Grandmaman is willing to your bride; you must cherish forever
an invitation to your mother's wedding . . .
O the legions of names that will never have faces, the cancers
that grew on them, as if they were the faces . . .
And the young sit uneasily, stiffly as wood, at the point
that the threads all somehow insist on coming back to.

But the young have intangible allies: the senses
waiting to blossom like deep horns into the skull
and open the echoing valleys; so the outside
arrives in a thunderous surf . . . One day a lilac
sprig sways, and you are shaken from head to foot with the vertigo
of *why here and now go on at all,* when you blink your eyes.
Then the bad old story is over, and the poem
begins, that goes nowhere, but only deepens and glows.

                    Have you felt this? the school rocked
                    to the roots, the floors weird planes and sliding—
                    the gulf of the future
                    that hides in bones, turning
                    all first loves' faces to statuary . . .
                    the love of the thought of your thought made
                    of green cells . . .

But how sluggish the blaze looks to those who are still in the story!
The boy who slouches, one leg tossed high over
the chair-arm, and answers with hateful overpoliteness,
his mind on negligees far as foam on the beaches of China,
seems hardly alive . . . As they try, so they think, to reach him
with barbed remarks; as they go on trying, his anger
fogs their lives with the deathliness they see in his.
O the endless summer coastal fog

of the photo they live in! the Fourth-of-July lights worming
the cataracts of my blind grandmother's eyes!

> So that, years later, the flashes
> catch at you oddly: was it really your great-
> grandmother who died dragged by
> a riding horse through the Bois de Boulogne?
> and her husband, the gentle
> composer, Ferdinand de Croze, who pined
> away and died within a year
> after leading Grandmaman
> through the ice caves up Monte Rosa?

And then you know you will live in a bare white room,
its splendors books and the covers of books, and tiptoe
against all that entangles you back and smaller—the musty
taste of cabbage, small flocks
listed in the chinks of the nomad rug—unless
you can imagine what is nowhere now, and make
the black dots of the photo buzz between, in rose.

ELEANOR ROSS TAYLOR

Pause, in Flight

Late August. The wind stays awake all night
Thinking of Autumn. The crickets wonder
Out loud about the future . . . Damn the past.
Damn the past . . . Fall is yonder,
The constellation we are travelling to.
No, we are where it is travelling to
From a distance, a time, long overdue,
Extinguished before the hunter put
The gun over his shoulder. Will these trees
Be the last to receive
This light?
        The crickets, apprehensive,
Give ear. This light, this autumn, this hunter
Comes already dead. Who
Flutters featherless into the leaves?

The Skipped Page

If she stayed on her knees long enough
Maybe somebody would tell her
What she was doing in this house
So long unvisited;
What the beds were doing, made,
That had so long untidily held *them*;
What the sunlight did
Belaying the grimy pane;
And who was that, out there,
Sitting on a child's chair
Near the woodpile, holding a cane,
Facing the winter clouds
With fake fearless gilded eyes.

And she debated, turning her rings,
The dead telephone,
And how she would answer it there,
There where the knife was already in tomorrow
And her plate crying to receive the carcass.

WILLIAM JAY SMITH

The Angry Man

"El sueno de la razon produce monstruous."

I

Reason slumbers; and in the terrible isolation of my anger I observe
a thousand monsters of the mind's making;

I wander on a moonscape exploring its tunnels, picking up bits and
pieces of the past

To hurl at growling beasts that sulk away half-seen; I gaze from a
steel cage out at a wall rimmed with dragon's teeth,
observation towers and aprons of barbed wire

Lacing the horizon; eyes peer through the night as through the
isinglass of old coal stoves;

I am a passenger on a ship in the shape of a carving block
bearing a cargo of bones;

I know the language spoken by cats and dogs, all peripheral tongues;
I invent new words, every syllable detailing disaster;

I am the King of Buttons, enriched by bottle-caps, profligate with
paper;

My voice goes out like a funicular over an abyss, and my hands
hang at my side, clenching the void;

My dreams are filled with bitter oranges and carrots, signifying
calumny and sorrow;

And when I awake the windows are outlined in creosote; a network of
pipes is thrown up around my room and water pours from a
yellow geyser in the plaster.

II

Reason slumbers; and I go where the world takes me—back upon
myself; and if I have slept, I awake, projected on a raft
into a soft green landscape

Where blanched concrete highways keep circling the hillsides in
        whalebone, drinking up the cars through the baleen formed by
        spiny trees against the sunset—

And I am the passenger hurled from the passing car, the driver
        swallowed by the black whale of the world;

And the journey ends where it began: the black whale's mouth opens
        around me into a pleated camera in which my eye is the lens—

And what I see is a world opening into other black mouths—
        gullet to gullet—lens to lens—

And what is recording is recorded, what is seeing, seen; and
        the giant shutter opens always on horror.

III

The monsters of the mind's making have begun their destruction
        and will carry it through;

They keep attacking, throwing iron hoops that encircle my
        ankles, thighs, chest

Until I am bound with iron rope and hung from a precipice; and the
        cliff is no cliff but a ceiling from which hairy roots
        dangle at my side—

Not roots but the branches of trees growing into the air by their
        roots—

Around them dream flowers twisting out—black roses, blue sun-
        flowers following a black sun—

Morning glories, dirt-colored blooms encircling mansarded
        basements—

Skylights opening out like trapdoors into gray cloud caverns in
        which birds dive downward like fish, and television aerials float,
        the skeletons of dangling kites—

Rivers are nailed above me, their bird-fish flying, teeth dragging
        the marbled water, and their debris lining a painted dome of
        tin cans, bottles, rusted and twisting knives;

A bloated piano like a black armadillo bores its way over the
  edges into a cloud

And cemeteries drift overhead like upturned trays held by frozen
  waiters.

IV

The black iron hoops snap and uncoil, coiling me upward, upright,
  backward in time and space;

I am alone in a courtyard in the middle of a desert, holding in my
  hands the coils that have become a whip.

It is dusk, and the air is alive with soft flying creatures;
    I snap the whip at them, looping their bodies, bringing
    them down until the stones of the courtyard are red.

And at last the air is quiet and no chirp or whimper is heard
    from any chink or crevice.

I climb the spiral stone steps to a room overlooking the desert;
    and I lie now on an iron coat watching the moon-white sand
    billow out in waves like the sea;

And the whip, having answered unreasoning reason, rests limp
    at my side—a tassel, a tail, a reed.

A Picture of Her Bones

I saw her pelvic bones one April day
After her fall—
Without their leap, without their surge or sway—
I saw her pelvic bones in cold X ray
After her fall.
She lay in bed; the night before she'd lain
On a mat of leaves, black boulders shining
Between the trees, trees that in rain pitched every which way
Below the crumbling wall,
Making shadows where no shadows were,
Writing black on white, white on black,
As in X ray,
While rain came slowly down, and gray
Mist rolled up from the valley.
How still, how far away
That scene is now: the car door
Swinging over above her in the night,
A black tongue hanging over
That abyss, saying nothing into the night,
Saying only that white is black and black is white,
Saying only that there was nothing to say.
No blood, no sound,
No sign of hurt nor harm, nothing in disarray,
Slow rain like tears (the tears have dried away).
I held her bare bones in my hands
While swathed in hospital white she lay;
And hold them still, and still they move
As, tall and proud, she strides today,
The sweet grass brushing against her thighs,
A whole wet orchard mirrored in her eyes;—
Or move against me here—
With all their lilt, their spring and surge and sway—
As once they did that other April day
Before her fall.

Venice in Fog

I

Fog in mid-December has descended on Venice; and the city wraps
itself around itself

Like the seahorses we have seen in the aquarium, tails linked,
twisting, turning,

Rising gently to the green surface of the water; the water of
Venice, a mirror,

Is held up on all sides so that the bridge reflected rises and
drifts toward us, a twisted turret,

And the city, lighter than goose down, is about to float through
the air—

Or rest, a hulk, a battleship stranded, gray on gray sand, green
barnacles encrusting

Its gray guns; the silver of the mirror is rubbed away so that
one looks not into, but through, the glass,

And moves in a carnival, where black masks wander up and down, and
the people wearing them

Are nowhere to be seen—they're lost in fog—and the buildings
come at you through holes in the masks;

Bodies—ghosts' bodies—brush by you in the mist; the Bridge
of Sighs is an eyelid

Lifted on a gray eyeball; and behind it a red boat light slowly
streaks with blood.

II

Saint Mark's bursts at us through fog, the mottled, humped face of
a bright tropical fish;

The Doge's Palace beside it rests on the intaglio of its pillars,
a stranded fish skeleton.

The *aqua alta* has subsided; in dim pools in the square the
pigeons huddle in the cold,

Flying apart of a sudden like a fringe of wool, purple threads
at their throats,

And one, frayed and battered, limps off toward the ruby glow of
a jeweled shop,

And, nuzzling its head against a column, falls over dead, its
mauve feathers the wet wisps of an old broom.

Fragments of buildings—architraves, cornices, pediments—fly
through the night

And here at our feet, a group of gondolas tied together sit, squat,
a row of black, muzzled dogs.

The lighted shops are so many bright boxes spilling out into the
night—gold, glass beads

Falling beside the water like multiple chains from the throats of
Venetian women.

Now in La Fenice—the fog behind us—we are inside the golden
box, and below us women in Minoan dress

Sing out their lives, and fall spent on amber rocks . . . And now
pink lobster, eel,

Layers of encrusted crayfish swim toward us through the gray light
where streetlights drift,

The blue-pink pods of the medusa . . . And our forks come down upon
the plate,

Cutting through the fog; we begin to bite into Venice, tasting
its hidden, sea-green sweetness.

III

Three days and the fog gives no sign of lifting (after three days
of fog it rains, they tell us) . . .

Cats go masked; white-veiled, bulging flower shops float off,
barges bearing the remnants

Of bridal festivities . . . I touch their perfume as they move
away; and from here in the room gaze down

On the bridge below and the shops beside it held in marbled water,
veins of mist cutting

Through it while my pen on the page cuts through veined layers
of consciousness . . .

Domes, arched windows rising toward me are bushes bent down with
snow and ice; and the saints from their niches

Fly out like birds, all saying: Life is neither nightmare nor dream
but dream and reality converging;

Heaven, as Blake knew, can be met with anywhere, and what cannot
be seen must be imagined and seen more clearly . . .

Here seven years ago I walked at night through the fog, my steps
echoing behind me;

My past life rose up unmasked before me; and even then I could
see your face—a face I had not yet seen—

Swim toward me—a bright fine-boned face parting the spray
before it, the figurehead of a ship . . .

And I gaze down into the fog, and hear behind me—echoing up
through my life—

Your steps on the stair; you come in, cold from your walk, and
toss your purple cape on the bed, its fur wet from the fog;

Your hair falls red about your throat; you turn from the gold room
and run the water in the bath,

Steam rising from it like fog; and below me footsteps echo on the
pavement; bell buoys clang in the distance . . .

You step from your warm bath and lie down beside me; my hand
moves over the nipples of your breast,

Down over the firm belly and rests on your thigh; as the mirror
breaks in a thousand pieces,

The room is all pomegranate and gold; the fog clears—parting
as if for the marriage of Venice with the sea—

And all that could not be seen is seen, all that was imagined, is, all that
was lost, found.

AMANDA BULLINS

Elliot's Return from the Offshore Oil Rigs of Louisiana

So you came back for your flower of Virginia.
As you watch water run from my eyes
To a delta of lines that have formed below them,
You ask what things I saw
That dug so deep while you were gone.
I say digging took me only to China,
Where I woke without an interpreter,
Having slept through time changes.
You would have all Baby tears freeze.
I want the lines that show how hard
The winter was without you here to freeze,
To stop tracking up my face.
When we leave my house together,
Thermal clothing occupies the cold,
Keeps it from us for a while.
Later, in your paid-for room,
You are jealous of the time I keep
Myself at your writing desk, away from you.
Somehow I wish you would cry or
Cry out. In silence you make
Constant Comment, as though orange
Peelings could stop all bitterness.
In Sweden men pour tea for women.
You try to tell me.

Flight

I remember how we found you that Sunday
At the chicken coop turned toolshed,
Where you had made a neat pile
Of your socks and your shoes
And sat poking them with a stick.

This time you left more evidence—
After flying home from the city seven hours
Too late to visit, I inspect your room
To gather what I can:
Your skis are here, an English book
Bought second hand, postcards from friends,
Barbells, gymnastics suit, one old guitar.

Station to station collect I hear
That you are fine and found a job
At some small airline running errands.

I read off every digit on our mother's face—
It tracks us like a cash register on a binge—
Her eyes are an open tally sheet that shows
One, two, three, four children changed
From copper ore to fool's gold.
I read that it's this wait before beginnings
That kills mothers, cripples sisters
Jumping brooks in two-four time.

I spend all day talking to a college freshman
Fresh from a Florida prep school.
I tell him it's too far to where you are,
And I repeat it. The fellow whispers,
"Are you in a trance?"

JOSEPH GARRISON

Reddish Knob: From the Firetower

It was dark, except for the moonshine,
And I thought of Hawthorne's diorama man
In "Ethan Brand" as the headlights just
Missed the curve and flooded the top
Of the mountain. Lovers, I thought.

I was glad they couldn't see me.
Sitting there on my bed, surrounded
By the blackening windows, watching them
With habitual intent.

What took me most at first is that they didn't
Plunder with their bodies whatever love they may
Have had. I watched them tumble from the car
And gasp for air.
I expected him to take her hand at least,
But he didn't and kept his frozen distance
As if he mistook her for a deer and couldn't
Bring himself to startle up the creature.

They came to the dark tower and
Slowly ascending, reached the open deck.
I felt the structure shudder
And saw the tight fist of his right hand spark
As his other arm encircled her.

But then he broke away, turned,
And looked toward me,
And I looked at him not seeing me
And wondered if the Knob could feel its bloodstone burn.

Moonset

Down the narrow stairs,
Past a drunk in tow.

By lanterns on courtyards,
By voices, trees, we went

Through shadows to the car.
We were cold then,

Like pairs of empty hands;
The loving had burned

To a buried end.
From behind a wall

The moon appeared,
Almost full, its light

Made whole within it.
It was setting, not rising,

At the driven road's edge;
But we saw it go.

R. H. W. DILLARD

Alligator Night

1.
"The horrid noise of their closing jaws, their plunging amidst the broken
banks of fish, and rising with their prey some feet upright above the water,
the floods of water and blood rushing out of their mouths, and the clouds of
vapor issuing from wide nostrils, were truly frightful."

—William Bartram

Alligator night, the moon
Mottled, scaled, the water
As still as old age, palms
Clack and chatter, the fish
Rise and fall in clear rings,
And the alligators slide
Down the mud, toes and sharp
Tail, move into the bay.

The eye of the reptile
Winks like the moon
Through thin clouds,
Is cold as a dead bird,
Will not leave you
To the dark alone.

Like old logs bumping
Down to the mill,
A dark convoy, secret
Submarines, the brothers
Of the sick shark,
The alligators come,
A symmetry, hungry order,
The one equation.

They scrub the planks
Of your boat, the hiss
Of their passing eyes,
Slick coins, tails
Stirring the bay water
Like scalding coffee,
A silence loud as artillery,
As a saint's death.

2. "For we are not pans and barrows, nor even porters of the fire and torch-bearers, but children of the fire. . . . "

—R. W. Emerson

Seed case and tidal water
Hard as blood, you strike
nail on stone and blossom
Into sulphur, into flame,
Blaze and sputter, hot fat,
Break light from your dark cells.

A flame casts shadows,
Hisses, snaps, slips
Smoke into the night air,
And eats away, like cancer
Gnawing on old bones,
Bruised flesh, heat
Of decay, the growth
Under your arm, hot
Tumor snarled in your brain.

And die,
Old web, worn out,
An echo in his eyebrow,
Cast of her eye, a trunk
Of suits, the medal,
A husk as dry as kindling,
As tinder, punk.

3. ". . . children of the fire, made of it, and only the same divinity transmuted and at two or three removes, when we know least about it."

— R. W. Emerson

"After this sight, shocking and tremendous as it was, I found myself some-what easier and more reconciled to my situation."

—William Bartram

There are cures:
The harsh salt, the acid,
Sharp knife, X ray,
The pills and bitter capsules,
Tubes, pulleys, the plastic
Arm, the borrowed heart.

And in the ashes, old fire,
You stir like a stiff bird
At dawn, stretch out,
And try your hurt, gland's
Drain, eye's squint, locked knee,
Burn in the healed nerve.

The day like a lizard
Swells in the sun, colors,
The bay empty as glass,
Palms like feathers,
The light as round
As a button, as a day,
As open.

The alligator in the park,
No sign in his grey skin
Of breath, his one eye
Closed, warm in a circle
Of pond and high fence,
Sleeps in the sun
Like a painful memory.

Rain

(After the Spanish of Jorge Luis Borges)

The afternoon produces a rain.

It also falls in the past.

You hear it. You remember the day
You first saw the color of a rose,
Saw the flower (you knew the name).

This rain closes the window,
But it opens tiny lenses in the screen
Of the room you knew, slicks the plums
On a bent tree that is no more.

This wet afternoon brings you the sound
You have been listening for:

Your father's voice, alive in the rain.

Limits

(After the Spanish of Jorge Luis Borges)

The rain holds you in like skin
Or a wall, steady, almost solid.
The brick walls through the trees
Move like dreams or memories.
Your eyes search for sharp things,
Objects with edges, lights like knives.
The day has lost all definition,
Is as closed as some dark lithograph.

You remember:
The rain of May, the rain of July,
The rain of ten years ago in the winter,
A whisper shared in the rain,
How the rain smashes on your shoes
Or its loose rattle on an umbrella,
Rain in weeds or across water,
The taste of rain, the smell,
How her skin is as slick and shiny
In the rain as an apple or plums.

You know:
There is a poem by Borges
You will never remember,
And a street (it curves down the hill)
That is forever closed to you,
At least one door (the knob once warm
With your hand) which you have closed
Until the end of the world.

I know a face which I seek in every stranger's,
Which I shall never see again.
I know there are books in my shelves
(They are all around me now)
Which I shall never open again.
This wet autumn closes my thirty-fourth year.
Death continues to blur and reduce me,
To reduce you as you read this page,
Steadily and as sure as rain.

Walking Home from the Raleigh Court Branch Public Library

I reach the first real page
of John H. Watson's reminiscences
Who took his degree in 1878.
The year is 1949, and I have only
a mile to go. I am walking home.

Sometimes today I want to loosen out
Like a large flag, possibly orange,
In an early April wind, and do.
But more often I remember
Walking home where I can really settle in.

RUDY SHACKELFORD

Entreaties

I went to the prince of nettles
and bowing before him
implored a crumb of pain

he said You are not worthy
to suffer Go stare
at the sun

but the sun had gone
into an unscheduled eclipse

I waited years at the drawbridge
for a ship which was never to pass

the harborman beckoned me Leap
had I trusted him
I wouldn't be drowning there in the sand

---

to the keeper of the bell tower
I ascended
the iron spiral of his inner ear

he stood draped in ropes
studying a table of changes

One spends a lifetime here
he said Preparing to ring the hour

RICHARD McCANN

Watching the Traveler

You are at the north border, startled,
afraid of cold weather. Nothing
will bless you. Two crows
are tearing at the sky behind you, which crumbles
like old paint. They'll dig through to what's theirs.

It is night. The wind
has smashed my front window, sent
the glass motes flying
like moths, white wings sailing
through the dark, bits
of loose paper, torn letters. Now
they lie scattered on the lawn, reflecting
the house lights.
The empty pane reflects

nothing, pulls at the great distance
you have traveled. You are headed
for Ottawa, old home where the highways
circle south again. At the border you stop,
turn your small pack out
on the steel table while a custom's man
pokes through it with a stick. The arctic dream
pulls you on to where hunted animals
drag themselves across ice to the sea.

Here it is March
and the cold contracts around us
like a ring. I go out back
to fill the last buckets with kerosene,
my skin tight as a frozen cloth. Slowly
I let the warm gas spill
on my hands, whiten the widening pores.
I go in to start the stoves. You will call tonight.
When you stop
the miles will spin out of you like breath.

You Ask Me How I'm Doing, I Tell You

History, memory, men, women. I sit at the picnic table with your children, watch them try to separate the blue clay from the red but it's all swirled in a circle and won't pull apart. I think they should make little animals and just forget it. A little paint, a little glaze: Who cares what's underneath? Last week I dreamed a man was scratching a screwdriver across the surface of things, just what I don't know.

A plate shatters and I put the pieces in a drawer, worthless. The problem's separation. I study your children's books, biographies of heroes, baseball, machines. Beneath every page something's been erased. Every picture's painted over. To cover a tattoo the old lines are used to start the new. A snake's tongue spreads to wings, an eagle. It must be more elaborate. In this book I see a gun quite clearly beneath a man's kind face. Inside a blender I swear I see a woman's not quite attached.

When you ask me how I'm doing I mention all this. Look, we're best friends, you say, why metaphor? In the kitchen I slam fruit into the blender and grind it to a pulp. I want to make big meals for everyone to eat. I want to fill the drawers with coupons and used foil. I want to cover things up.

My parent's house: clear vinyl covers on brocade, dresser scarves, diplomas framed under pictures, toaster, toilet paper hidden in crochet. My mother, unable to untangle a gold chain, drives to the jeweler's. I see this house like a real estate ad: l.v. b.r. c/h and air. Abbreviations separate the function from the name. The old snapshots fade, there is only a sense of what the weather was. The lovers on the hill grow indistinct, rocks, stumps. In the darkroom they're submerged beneath a stain, then solarized.

Groceries, laundromats, perfect for murders, memories. The codes of shoppers are clear: I want this, do you read me? You shove the throw rugs in the washer and I confide the dream where I bend over myself with black thread and needle. My small punctures are bubbling like a burst tire. I sew myself up. All around us the washing machines hit spin. Look, I say, your children's doll is missing an arm, a lank of hair. Who takes care of this sort of thing? Who do I call? You think I'm domestic like every man should be. I think there's blood somewhere and someone ought to wipe it up.

MARGARET GIBSON

Castings

1.

As we were sitting there
with the wine and the oysters

our words unraveling

Beethoven's adagio darkened
            in the air

            a steady reproach

no anger
I remember the vibrato
                    listening
                    to all the voices

the knot in my throat
tightening

2.

"There is something in you
(you say)
            that causes anger
            that is deaf to reproach
            It maintains itself

In you there is
a well without a rope or bucket or dipper
Down the corridor of the well
I see a small coin of light
the glint of a nebula"
                    Your anger strikes across a sky
                    the skin blue of plums
                    It bruises and broods

        Out of the yellow vase
        on the mantelpiece
        voices lift
        "You are cold"

3.

Sometimes I see us walking down a curve of space an arc of a wide road
covered with footprints with shards of pottery beakers with something I can't
distinguish there's a risk at the point in the road the road bends like the ear
in a question mark your sentences enter my mouth become my own guess-
work sometimes we enter the room and perch like ming vases like dynasties
on the mantelpiece sometimes we are knives sometimes we advance steadily
each of us wears a thick black belt each of us holds in the cups of our hands
bruises which tremble like water like milk as the music darkens the road
deepens we vanish the branches go blue the rim sharpens

4.

The vase on the mantelpiece fades
Quietly you come into view
stargazer   woodsman
bringer of cordwood   apples
            blue plums   yellow pears
You give and give and give
You'd break stone into bread
if you could
            I try to chart your need

At night we trace the broken
constellations broken stones
You point out the path of the swan
You trace the rings of Saturn
on my fingers
            You slip through
You say I am never satisfied
You want to say: ease my pain
You give and give and give
                        and we still are
                        as distant as
                        these provisions are
                        from our need

Asleep in the firelight
asleep in my arms
you turn and turn
            I know in your dreams
            you are Orion
            and I am a rook
            splashed with blood

5.

Quietly you begin to speak
                    There are ashes in our throats
                                        (you say)
                    There are snakes' eyes in the evening dust

Agreed: there's a risk
                    we scatter and circle
                    we search for the lost
                    scent ripe and extinct

                    each voice has its cast
                    or contrivance or death
                    mask what you will
Agreed: there's a risk

Beethoven's adagio darkens
in the air
The lover turns away his head
The potter turns his wheel

And I am the shadow sun cast off from me
I walk out to the field
leaving no footprint
no rag on the thorn

Out of the yellow vase on the mantel
voices lift
                    descanting

Out of the pines wind bears the body
the ripening pollen across the fields

PETER FELLOWES

What Got Through

The warm palm on his mind,
in she goes, in where he is,
to poultice down—not
fast enough, faster
they must till again
from dysfunction, night inklings,
to love himself he has a mind,
she from untoward closehandedness,
they go down to the bottom,
the scolded skin, there concentrate.

Still between his lengths, strung
with the strain, ordinary
as clothesline, and stray
else eaten front first, she says,
good, blood branches
she may shake down, throwing
her weight to, sticking to,
till down the hatch,
fantastic, how for good
she loves him up, she's stuffed.

No matter, he puts the more instead
his mind to the very hill
of her, not to be grasped,
reaching in to furnish
wry angles out, no, but pressing
his forehead exactly to the hill,
the harder to stamp her in, the quicker
not to lose track or covet
any meaning but this kindness
is on his mind, she loves him.

To the Farmer of Milk Cows

A crow will bend their ears
back to it, crying
night upon them all,
a man will stop them dead,
then down again, they draw
the alfalfa from the earth
and mill it into milk.
Their shiny eyes look sideways
down the long, smooth snout
of simpleness of heart.

When the night dome
has been laid, when the cold wind
combs the field, they browse
the fencing for a break,
but let the morning
find them joined to the yoke,
their nostrils steaming,
piss jetting from their rears,
and while they mash grain forage, let
the udder gloves desire.

For them, love keeps the gentlest
and the swiftest darts of all,
and drops the round cow
with a drooling bite
flat in the straw, or tucks her bones
sweetly in a culvert's weeds. For love,
then, farmer, forbear the club,
till her dug wags at the grass
three summers dry and the crow
grows lean upon her dung.

DABNEY STUART

Sticks and Stones

1

This pencil moves on the page
White as a swan's quill,
Making its music,
Playing its tunes
With no more noise than a swan
Makes moving
Over the rippling lake.

Three hundred years ago
Men wrote
With the feathers of birds
And courtly fingers
Picked Morley's airs
From the lute with plectra
Made from the feathers of birds.

2

This pencil, Venus 2,
This unwieldy timber
You can start a fire with,
This shaving
That writes *tree,*
This small stick
That bears the name of a goddess
And can write *love*
As cleanly as a knife
Cuts the names of lovers
Into the bark of trees,
This light toy
That can form a word
Heavy as *stone,*
Leaves its marks on this white paper
With no more noise
Than a pebble
Thrown by two lovers
In late afternoon
Makes, sinking
Through the water
Of a lake, played on
By the shadows of trees.

3

The river in its narrows
Moves on over the stones,
Riffles, moves on over
The stones, reflects the sun,
Moves on, covering the stones
Played on by the shadows of trees.

A fisherman's rod
Moves through its arc, the fly
Settles on the water,
Drifts through the sun,
Plays in the shadows of trees,
Moves on over the stones
To the end of the line, jerks,
Drifts, jerks.

The fisherman's blood
Hums in its veins,
Moves on over his bones.

4

The smallmouth bass
Hovers over the pebbles
In the moving water,
Watching the fly jerk,
Drift, jerk.
Dappled, motionless
As a stone, he waits
On his hunger, and will rise
For the fly in one
Invisible swiftness,
As the fisherman's need
Rises silently to words
Through the depths of his dreams.

5

Scattered along the shore
Among the stones
Untouched by the water
The bones of birds
Lie, bleached whiter
Than this page, played on
By the shadows of trees.

6

Above the still lake water
And the moving stream,
Above their beds of stones,
The wings of birds
Make no more noise
Than this pencil moving
Across this page, leaving
Its weight of words,
Make no more noise
Than the bass striking
The fly, no more
Than the fly drifting,
Jerking, drifting, no
More than the fisherman's need
Rising through his sleep
Leaving his dreams
Through words that seem
In their silence
To fly under the sun
Nest in the shadows of trees.

Goshen Pass: Winter

for Henry Sloss

Seen through the windshield of a car
Winding from one end of this pass to the other
The mountains seem to move, as a half-open door
Moves when you move, revealing more, or less,
Of the room beyond it. Yet the man who starts in this pass
Walking
Finds his hike entirely mountainous
Finds nothing he did not see from his car,
Though he may learn that if the mountains move
He does not move them.
                         Seen through the windshield of a car
Parked anywhere in this pass
Sheer rhododendron, bare oak
And dogwood, the monotonous evergreens
Cedar and fir, all seem rooted in stone
Shelf after shelf. Gross limpet shells
Of ice suck the receding ledges
Where fold and scarp poise upward on themselves
To the high ridges. Yet the man who sits in this pass
Staring, is blind
To this, the face of it

The way the mountains move

And in a time that is beyond his means
They will have outstripped his climbing, moved to a height
Visible only from the single island
Poised in the river moving over its stones
—the stones of the mountains—its singing caught
By the walls of its passage, increased,
As though it were tuned to their motion
As well as their own.
                  And spring,
That dubious season, has nothing to do with this motion,
Will not in his time bring
Either delicate feet to these raw terraces
Subduing them, or those others rehearsing their ring
Who come to bless stone, and whom stone blesses.

For now this is his pass
And he has come to it with his boots on
Faithful to his season, a driving age
Whose ghosts will not be seen dancing beneath that tree
Stone-rooted on the solitary island, willing a heritage
Of celebration and austerity.
Whatever he sees now he sees for the same reason
That the clearest pane of glass
May show him
Not the aspect of a particular place
But only, reflected, his own face.

Love Letter

He found
A single feather in the sprung trap

He took it home
And with it
Wrote to his wife

I make this with part of what escaped
You know the style

I have always imagined
A calendar retrieving its pages

A stone house with a spring
A rune scratched on a wall in its cellar
A hearth

The light here quivers
As if the wind were in it

I make this with part of what is free

When he gave it to her
She said, without reading it

I have something to show you

Come to the window

Vision

Three years after the fire died
I huddled in the fireplace

The ashes freezing
The flue leaking my share of the odor
Of billboards

All the highways led here
Following me

I thought the room
Empty
And saw you
Leaning against the abrupt mantle

Miles off

Your face stale with longing
Staring through me into the stone

Snorkeling in the Caribbean

In the second place, they live without fragility.
If they are eaten they are eaten, and that's that.

You cannot imagine the abundance
Of life without consciousness, the risk is too great.
Consequently, all
Is not one. There is nothing besides diversity.
Why else do you suppose men find it difficult
To live in harmony? The one that comes
Out of the many is death.

                  By the same token, they eat
Or not, according to what is available.

Would you live on lice and roaches?
Would you choose to starve? Is there any accounting
For taste?

If your son's foot were pierced by the spines of a sea urchin
Would you go on your knees before him and piss on the wounds?
Or would you bind him up and seek out the undertaker?

                  Even in August
The weather is temperate, there is a constant breeze that dries
Your linen in fifteen minutes, and the cocktails are on the house
Mondays.
          Who could ask for anything more?
                              They don't.
They swim,
They eat,
They move away from me, they move
Away.
        If peace exists anywhere it exists here, under
Water
            —my ears fill with it, it leaks into my mask—
                        where
What little that is asked is answered,
Always, under
Water
        in the second place

                              which I would raise
Like a goblet—this small bay containing everything,
More or less—to you, brave child who will not weep,
Whose pain my urine eases, who learns to swim
Behind a mask like mine.

JAMES EVERHARD

Miracles

---

1 Waking the Dead

A butterfly lights
upon your lips. What
you were going to speak
you forget. The dead
rise out of the ground
on wings mistaking your
silence for the sign,
but too late, the dead
are rising, weeping with
joy, like moths
out of the night
filling the air with
their dust, running
into the headlights of cars
crying, "We are saved,
we are saved."

2 Stigmata

You hold the stigmata
in your palms as though
they are pearls. You
slip soft gloves
over them, the gloves'
palms bleed. You
touch the face of a girl.
A stigma blooms on her forehead,
the third eye with which
she sees the face of god.
You touch a stone.
It bleeds like a sheep's heart
tossed out to the dogs
in the snow. You
pass your hands through
the wounds in a mirror,
cross over to a
solitary shore, let loose
the stigmata like birds
into an open field.

3   Walking on Water

Into the desert
you trek
sucking a cactus thorn;
where your feet touch down
sand melts into water.
You walk on until
like the drowned or meditative
you drift down into yourself.
The desert opens
a single blue eye.

4   Curing the Lame

You touch the shriveled
leg with your trembling,
guided hand. Paralysis,
a stone, drops to the ground
with the faithful weeping
in witness. You touch
the leg of a horse, a
hunched-back beggar.
You journey to kings,
are welcomed into
the leper dens.
You touch the leg
of a table, a flute,
a needle. The lame come
dancing toward you
to be healed.

For Marcie

---

the last night
you came to the house
had pizza and
after an uneasiness
that wasn't going to end
i told you i was no
lover boy remembering
what warren beatty said
somewhat unconvincingly to
faye dunaway but
remembering also how things
never ran smoothly between us
the night you called me
and confessed you'd
taken more speed
after i tried unsuccessfully
to break it up but
was still having trouble
with my male ego
our first time together
in bed i pounced on you
kissing feeling knowing
if it didn't work out
i could excuse it for being
the first time and all
but later, again . . .
and you asked me about my fantasies
to try and help i couldn't
tell you they were all with men
we decided not to rush things
i knowing they would come
to a dead halt . . .
the first night
afterwards not sleeping
but both of us pretending,
you in my arms
a cat on the windowsill
your roommate and another man
in the next room in the
quiet of that house

a fog creeping through the orchard
into which morning birds
disappeared one by one.

KATE JENNINGS

Baking at the Beach

Everyone else is on the beach. I'm in the kitchen, taking pride
in precise measures and care not to run out of sugar, oil, yeast.
I walk the narrow galley, done to a turn and sweating under my bikini,
making bread, heating meat, chopping and slicing with my small sharp
knife, shoving the point in and peeling, dicing, mashing. My hair
sifts through the still air like the flours and meals I deal with,
settling on my bare back in stiff pikes of heat. Electricity sparks
from my raised hands.

The crowd I cook for surges in, talking and shrieking and reaching
out to me for second helpings, their voices peaking at a pitch my
fever's never reached. A man smacks my backside and tells me I'm
all woman. A real woman.

A real woman! I lean against the sink and close my eyes, faint with
hunger. The mirror shoots back a blank face, a mug as empty as a clean
cup. The newspaper crackles and greases transparent at my touch. I
should be on the beach. I should strut the sand at high noon. Instead
I creep out after dark to the pier where they tell me a shark's
beached, and I stand and stare at his gray flesh, sickened to see
small bones gone useless. As I watch I wish he'd hump and shuffle
his slow weight and slope off down the pier, inching the harsh night
that blackens and dots itself with stars, pricks of protest and grief.
I think of you, my sister.

You claim you can cook as though it's a talent; you say you feed a
family of four on nothing a month, but they could be fed better on
less. The man you boast of couldn't touch me and could be stolen
from you with dazzle and returned to you

frazzled and dizzy and stunned. I crouch by meat, my knees spread.
I'm no lady and this vacation's over. The tricks our mothers taught
us don't hold water. We can paint these eyes like lizards' and
smirk and birth to hold a soul as husband but a smacked backside's no
reward for our labors. The trap's lock rots; this escape's as easy to
make as dinner. I squint at a moon who's no more woman than I.
Heartened, I return to the kitchen to make shark soup, a stew of
greased gristle, a last stab to leave to nourish the men I've left.

DAVID JEDDIE SMITH

The Lost Hunter in the Dismal Swamp

Often I think I hear you thrashing under the wheel
of the cicadas and locusts, fighting the hard suck
of the swamp, battered pipe in your yellow teeth,

a net of scars on your cheeks gouged by unseen thorns.
I watch from my cropped field where peanuts urge slowly
toward the ancient trees, but darkness comes unchanged.

The swamp doesn't change and Washington's Ditch flows
as brown as Cherokee blood to Lake Drummond, though tourists
take home swatches of moss and small bears, hungry, go

through garbage the city dumps like flies. It is madness
to think you will ever emerge from this lost ocean, bone
knife in your hand, lean as a cottonmouth: the last man

to hunt the Great Swamp and live. But myths, muy hombre,
let us live with the gnats, mosquitos, translucent skins
of dead civilizations that doom us to the long hours

in cold light. I think of you in a pure corner of darkness
where the rank, webbed net of time is stayed by ancient
impenetrable cypress, your knife marks deep in wood, like

a language of survival. At any time they could find you,
huddled like a fawn in the clasp of deep roots, your skin
turned to the mottled colors of peat, your eyes mossed,

narrowed at the light where you surface. At dusk I hear
the swamp's festering songs, unchanged, waiting, while
Drummond glitters like a starry knife hollowing soft pine.

The Wives at Old Point Comfort

On the last day they wake, like knives,
all knees and ribs and teeth cutting
the fishermen free of the sheets
and the flies banging on the screens
where the summer is storming.

Each one pretends her eyes are closed
as she stares at the man she must remember
at this table, before the hated bacon,
the plate of bleeding, dazzled eggs.

In her belly she feels him rise, thinks
how his sandy hair is more breathable
than water, finer than the sand
water is always stealing in the coves.
She must remember to remember his hair.

In the last darkness of that night
they rise with the fishermen and bear
to the boats a terrified, womanish odor,
women who must fall back through fields

where the leaves hiss with hot winds
and children practice the curses
a father leaves like a hand on a breast.
On the last day sorrow blisters her mouth

as she remembers loving him, turning back
at the black docks, the fish scales
everywhere, tiny jewels, egg chips
like pockets of sunlight on her legs,
transparencies she must remember always.

GARY SANGE

Lighthouse Keeper

I am rooted to a cliff
that can wreck what I warn.
In the sweeping light I spot
each time too late the mast

of a slowly vanishing
schooner half under
the beach—winded, split
by a cargo of fathoming sand.

For years I've been the only
survivor. My light is run now
by remote control.
I oil machinery
and wait to repair.

A dark hub in an oval room
I feel turned
by the spoke of light.
I am tired of being alert,
tired of keeping my eye out
for something irregular on the waves.

No more. It is late.
I must complete my dream
of schooners going down.

QUENTIN VEST

Serein

We are standing under the trees
and it is getting dark.
I hear the sound of rain too fine to see.
We have been walking across the lawns
unable to get each other's attention.

I have watched you come to the glass
      the wall I have never touched
trying to see what is on the other side.
I said nothing when I saw your tears.
You could not embrace the glass.
I would know you anywhere.
We have never looked at each other.
When the fine rain falls like this
we stand under the trees.
It is getting dark.
The rain continues to fall
      there is nothing on the other side of the rain
but the sky is clear.

The sky is not clear
The sky is full of stars.
When we look into space
we say there is no limit to the light.
We say there is no darkness
      only light that has not reached us yet.
When we look into space
the rain continues to fall.

I am standing under the trees.
It is dark now. You have never seen
your bruised arms, your thin shoulders.
You are like a child, hopelessly loving
the father who has abandoned him.
I would follow you anywhere
but you stand here waiting for me.

The Darkhouse

I get tired of it.
I decide to do something.
I move to Brittany.
On the cliffs of Quiberon
I build a darkhouse.

I fit it with a lamp
so powerful the black
sweep of its beam is visible
morning and afternoon,
all up and down the coast,
far out beyond Belle-Isle.

Every day, all day I man
the tower, just in case.
If only one is saved
it will be worth it.

BRUCE GUERNSEY

Houses We Lived In

I.

The first was dark brown.
We had a big yard then
but my father, a soldier, was never home.

Always, in the living room,
the heavy drapes were drawn.
In their shadows my grandmother's jade chows
guarded, like gargoyles, her teakwood tables.
Built like Buddah, she worshipped the Orient.

The kitchen was pure white.
A crucifix cloaked with palms
hung by the clock, next to the table.
The icebox hummed its hymn.
At breakfast my grandfather,
his right ear a suction cup,
listened for news of the war.

II.

The second was the yellow of the sun.
I watched my father, high on the ladder,
his brush filling in the sky.

The attic was a turret, my secret,
where draped in my father's uniform,
I pledged to keep the Reds away.

Then once, while looking for his medals
in the bureau in their bedroom
I found a slick, round, cold piece of rubber.

III.

The third had no color at all,
stark as stone in the hot sun of June
when I first came home from college.

We sat in the den,
our words twisted by gin
and the war I wouldn't fight

At dinner that night
the last word slipped like a knife:
the blood of the meat pooled on our plates.

IV.

This is my own,
a deep blue house near the ocean.

My cat walks the battlements of our picket fence.
My wife raises fennel in the window box.
My song sings in his swing from the maple.

The long war is nearly over.
In the fall I'll go hunting with my father.

JOHN ALEXANDER ALLEN

A Word to a Father, Dead

Whatever it was that went wrong—the stove aflame
In the kitchen with a sudden rage to burn
The house down; or the shower madly bent
On flooding us out, when stubbornly the drain
Backed up and nothing you did could shut the water
Off—whatever it was, it worried you;
And though your faith was perfect, in your hand
Buckets wickedly would turn to sieves.

I believe you were ready to call it quits
When something in your heart, a part of you not
To be gotten along without, went wrong. I believe
You were ready then, when all was said and done,
For death, unsent-for though it was, to come;
Willing, as anyone might have been, for someone
Different, in event of fire and flood,
To be on hand, to do the worrying.

Familiar now with death, whatever it is,
You will have forgotten the old bizarre concoction
Of the kitchen, the old routine of plumbing's
Comic imperfection. Still, I've not
Forgotten how you told me, in a dream,
"I'm sorry, sorry," and I knew your flesh
Had only pity for its own, and held
Itself alone accountable for grief.

But no. I've kept my hand in, in the kitchen;
Being a tenant, needn't worry my head,
Though a rusty pool appear beside the grumbling
Water heater. What's a landlord for?
Whatever it is that's happened since we met,
You're used to it. I'm getting the hang of time
In time for what comes next. Whatever it is,
Don't worry. Don't, whatever it is, be sorry.

HENRY TAYLOR

Riding a One-Eyed Horse

One side of his world is always missing.
You may give it a casual wave of the hand
or rub it with your shoulder as you pass,
but nothing on his blind side ever happens.

Hundreds of trees slip past him into darkness,
drifting into a hollow hemisphere
whose sounds you will have to try to explain.
Your legs will tell him not to be afraid

if you learn never to lie. Do not forget
to turn his head and let what comes come seen:
he will jump the fences he has to if you swing
toward them from the side that he can see

and hold his good eye straight. The heavy dark
will stay beside you always; let him learn
to lean against it. It will steady him
and see you safely through diminished fields.

Burning a Horse

> "We watch him burn—hoof, hide, and bone."
> —James Seay

Riding on a flatbed wagon, carrying with us
    an ax, pitchforks, a coil of heavy rope,
    and a five-gallon can of kerosene,

we went to the back meadow that afternoon,
    driven to desperate measures
    by the stench that hung on the still air,

dead air that lay like fog in the valley
    around us, not enough motion in it even
    to carry buzzards whose random glide

might have brought them to the body
    of the Percheron that festered on the grass
    where we had dragged him after he had died.

We spent an hour cutting brush from fallen trees,
    carrying it to where the horse lay bulging
    in the sun; we hooked him to the tractor

and pulled him over the pile of brush,
    to get it under him, then soaked
    the brushpile and his body with the kerosene.

I threw a match into the trembling vapors
    that rose from the fuel and from the rotting
    horse, then dropped back as the explosion

blasted us with the smell of burning hair. Slowly,
    one patch of skin, then another, burned through
    to let the gas escape and blaze like a blowtorch,

but the flames died down too soon, and we could hear
    the flesh speaking, one of the men said, as
    a cornfield does, growing after a hard rain.

We ran up to the pyre with more brush, holding
    our breath as we used pitchforks to place
    the dry sticks where they seemed needed most,

and then saw fire catch the wood, the flesh,
    and saw black smoke so thick and heavy
    that it hid us from each other; it crawled

down the meadow a few feet above the ground,
    the smell we held our breath against
    tainting everything it touched. Burning at last,

the horse was blackening and shrinking into the tall
    meadow grass; and then, before us, there,
    from coals that had caught hold in the horse's bones,

we saw a horse, made whole, with heavy flesh
    and shining skin, rippling against the pull,
    rising from the grass around the dying fire,

his new hoofs shod, his mane flying, rising
    from the coals and moving in a smooth
    and dangerous way; he traveled down the meadow

at a sweeping gallop, wrapped in something
    like a flame, light and heat around him
    that did not flicker or drop from him as he disappeared.

The sun rolled down the hill above a meadow,
    and in the dusk a wind came up.
    We strained our eyes, but the horse was gone,

moving perhaps beyond the stand of willow trees
    at the upper end of the meadow, carrying
    the light around him into darkness beyond our view.

We turned to look at the spot where the fire
    had been, listening for the crackling
    of smoldering bones, but all we heard

was our own blood and breath, and the sound
    of the wind that must have carried him away. Ashes
    lifted slowly in that wind, like heavy wings.

ANNIE DILLARD

Feast Days

Thanksgiving — Christmas

Part I

Three things are too wonderful for me;
   four I do not understand:
   the way of an eagle in the sky,
      the way of a serpent on a rock,
   the way of a ship on the high seas,
      and the way of a man with a maiden.

Today I saw a wood duck
in Tinker Creek.
In the fall flood, look
what the creek floats down:
once I glimpsed
round the edge of a bank
a troupe of actors
rained in from Kansas
dressed for comedy.
The flood left a candelabrum
on the lawn.
With a ten-foot hook
we fished from the creek
a bunch of bananas, a zither,
a casket of antique coins.

Or:
in the creek I found a log,
a tree trunk rotted halfway open.
Lord, lover, listen:
   I remember kissing on the stair
   dancing in the kitchen—
I crumbled the wet wood away.
Inside the trees a row of cells had grown,
sealed chambers, smooth, elongate.
I slit one open, found a book
hand-bound in yellow thread:
a child's book of wildflowers
sketched in ink
and washed with watercolors.

Come take a walk, you said.
And if I reached out
my hand could feel your shoulders move,
thin, under your shirt.
What newness, what surprises!
Once I dug a hole to plant a pine
and found a ruby, growing on a stone.

One thing we've got plenty of
here on the continents
is soil. Out of the soil
the plants are taking substance, edges,
like a tomato moving on its stake,
ten pounds of tomatoes, and the ground
blowing them up like balloons.
We walk on the soil
here on the continents
among the plants, and eat.

Thanksgiving: the men
are watching the game.
I wash, and dry, and dream:
I dream of a firelit room,
a tipi of eighteen buffalo hides,
of skins on the floor
and smoke curling up
the bark of the trunk of the lightwood lodgepole pine.

The Mandans in North Dakota
along the Missouri, prayed:
Go, flying birds, to the southern horizon,
to the old woman who never dies.
Return at the end of winter.
Carry sunshine, carry water
On your broad backs.
And in your beaks,
and in your beaks
bring her blessing like a berry
to the crops you symbolize:
"The wild goose to the maize,
the wild duck to the beans,
the wild swan to the gourds."

Thanksgiving, creation:
outside the great American forest
is heaving up leaves and wood from the ground.

Inside I stand at the window, god,
with your name wrapped round my throat like a scarf.

Today I've been naming
the plants of the southern forest:
arrowwood, witherod,
hobblebush, nannyberry,
and the loblolly, longleaf
and shortleaf pine.

Lean through the willow, look
upstream, and see what's floating down!
I see camels swimming
with long-lash, golden eyes.
I see trunks and telescopes floating,
a canopied barge with silk scarves flying,
a peacock on each post
and three crowned kings inside.
Kaspar, Melchior, Balthazar,
I suspect you're on to something.

You tell me your dream
and I'll tell you mine.

I dreamed I woke in a garden.
Everywhere trees were growing;
everywhere flowers were growing,
and otters played in the stream, and grew.
Fruit hung down.
An egg at my feet
cracked, opened up,
and you stepped out,
perfect, intricate lover.

Part II

Woman, why weepest thou?
Whom seekest thou?

December, and all the dark rains.
The apples in the cellar
are black, and dying inside their skins
they pray all night in their bins
but nobody listens:
they will be neither food nor trees.
Outside in the city
the cop wants to dig out his earmuffs,

the orange ones,
and if it were snowing he might,
but it's only rain.

God send us the springtime lamb
minted and tied in thyme
and call us home, and bid us eat
and praise your name.

God am I smug when they talk about Belsen.
I've never killed anyone in my life!
I simple betray:
let the phone ring,
seal a typed letter,
say to the girl in the courtyard
"I never saw him before in my life,"
call a cab, pull on gloves,
and leave. And leave you,
and leave you with the bill.

"Home," I say to the cabby,
"home, driver, to Tinker Creek.
It's in Virginia."
And he says, "Sorry, honey,
you can't get there from here."
"Then driver, please," I say,
"put me to bed."

Take a hot bath; take
a cold shower.
In your mouth stick
a silver spoon
so you don't crack.

Today you hurt your hand
on the fireplace.
Tonight a Chinook
rose up, from the south.
And my mouth
stuck shut,
my belly shook,
my eyes blinked hot,
and I went to the window.

There, stalking the lawn,
white tipis, wraithlike, ranged.

A smell of blood burned up.
The moon bruised down.
Antlers hung in the trees.
A thousand tipi doors lashed back
void, like riven graves.

And in the creek
in Tinker Creek
a sky-high blackened hull rose up:
a red-stacked ocean liner, sailing upstream.

They're on the roof,
naked, but I hear them.
I remember reading
in my room, just reading,
and shutting the book
and looking up
and missing you, missing you
and reading the paper again.
There's no freedom in it
or in fear:
my heart's not mine.
Once I went to the door
and an old black woman was there
in a clown suit
and a clown's peaked hat
and she carried a brown cloth bag.
Once an ape trailed through the hall
in my nightgown.
Once I surprised in the bathroom
the last of the Inca kings,
tall Atahualpa,
in his hand-stitched batskin robe.

Don't worry, I said,
it's all right, I said,
and ducked.

Oh, I've been here and there
around the heart—
a few night spots, really,
the kind that call themselves "Rathskellers,"
dim-lit, always changing hands,
and frequented on Sundays.
By the regulars:
mother in mink on the bar,

father looking up the grate to the sidewalk,
babies battling on the floor,
some sort of red-eyed monk
with a black-eyed mynah bird,
a clown (that clown!)—
and you.
variously,
weeping at the piano;
eating flyblown meat with a spoon;
swirling a beer and saying
"Marry me"; or
"I read your letter
(diary, palm)"; or
"You don't understand."
And then always,
Goodbye
(so long, take care)
remember?
And then I leave.
I'm always the one who leaves.

God send us the springtime lamb
minted and tied in thyme
and call us home, and bid us eat
and praise your name.

Part III

> And the captain of the Lord's host
> said unto Joshua, Loose thy shoe
> from off thy foot; for the place
> whereon thou standest is holy.

I love with my hand, not my heart.
When I draw your face
my fingers trace your lips.
Crossing a page, my hand keeps
contours; I know that art
is edges.
I touch when I type.
With every finger's tip
I travel the weave of the given.
Hand me a pencil,
cut off my head,
and I will draw you heaven.

Thank you, Squanto,
for the tip.
I knew something smelled funny in Iowa:
all that haddock, under the corn.

Mound builders,
basket makers,
cliff dwellers:
all are gone to the sandhills.
Remember Sand Creek!
Remember Wounded Knee!
Remember how to fish?
You may have my salmon rights
to Tinker Creek.
Just keep off the roof:
it's coming up Christmas.
Under the water the wood duck
feels with his foot in the creek.

By day I cook, and we eat.
At night your hand curls over my head,
curls into my hair as you sleep.
Hands curl up
like leaves. My hand curls up
from the fire to the tipi top
and out.
My hand curls down
the wood duck's throat.
In the curl of my hand I hold corn.

I kick through a forest of hands
by Tinker Creek. The sassafras hands
wear mittens: the tuliptree hands
demand money; "Wait!" cry the fraying hands
of a frivolous silver maple,
"I love you!"
A cottonwood hand floats down the creek
on its back, like Ophelia.

And deep on the banks of the creek
some hands uncurl;
some hand unleaf, and damply become
rich water,
wild and bitter perfume,
and loam, where bluets will bloom.

So your hand, asleep in my hair,
takes root, and flowers there.

Let me mention
one or two things about Christmas.
Of course you've all heard
that the animals talk
at midnight:
a particular elk, for instance,
kneeling at night to drink,
leaning tall to pull leaves
with his soft lips,
says, alleluia.

That the soil and freshwater lakes
also rejoice,
as do products
such as sweaters
(nor are plastics excluded
from grace)
is less well known.
Further:
the reason
for some silly-looking fishes,
for the bizarre mating
of certain adult insects,
or the sprouting, say,
in a snow tire
of a Rocky Mountain grass,
is that the universal
loves the particular,
that freedom loves to live
and live fleshed full,
intricate,
and in detail.

God empties himself
into the earth like a cloud.
God takes the substance, contours
of a man, and keeps them,
dying, rising, walking,
and still walking
wherever there is motion.

At night in the ocean

the sponges are secretly building;
by day in a pharmacy drawer
capsules stir in their jars.
Once, on the Musselshell,
I regenerated an arm.
Shake hands. When I stand
the blood runs up.
On what bright wind
did god walk down?
Swaying under the snow,
reeling minutely,
revels the star-moss,
pleased.

And to all you children out there with Easter bunnies
I would like to say this:
if they are chocolate, eat them.
If they are living, tuck them in your shirt.
There's always unseasonable weather.
Hose down the hutches.
For a special treat
to brighten up their winter
offer the early shoots of the wild American orchid,
the lady's tresses,
in either of three varieties:
the slender, the hooded, or the nodding.

ANNE WINTERS

Day and Night in Virginia and Boston

After three months, Virginia is still a frontier.
Late at night, I close the door
on my husband practicing Mozart, the dishpan fills
and the network affiliates sign off one by one.
Now the country stations, tuning up like crickets
on radios in scattered valley kitchens:
Har yall this evenin folks!
(Wanting to say "I'm real fine" I whisper "Wow.")
Got your Green Hill chicory perkin'? An army
of women, straightened and ironed and blued
like Picasso's ironer—jerking coffeecups
back with one gesture, hips pressed to sinks.
Their suspendered husbands are reading—the paper? the Bible?
And it's *Jesus for you and for me,* till midnight—the anthem—
and one soaped hand jerks out, and their lighted lives recede
to kitchens on the moon's dark side, Mozart rising . . .
Daytimes, in post office, gas station, greasy spoon,
I don't see them anywhere, it makes me nervous.
Black faces down here look "colored."
I am afraid of the other, red faces.

Take my first job in Boston,
the outgoing typist said, "You've got
to know the foms, we use so many foms."
And I said *O why farms?*
I thought law firms had *torts.*
A tort, I thought, was like *vous avez tort.*
But I was wrong about the farms,
and after the Cardinal's Vietnam speech
one of the girls said, "Think you're smat with that accent?"

Still, nothing soothes me, sometimes,
like American voices, softened with distance,
with nearness, as murmurs in a darkened Greyhound:
"It sure has been a scorcher." "Where you folks from?"
I keep yawning, lightworlds off in the dark . . .
Sometimes my lonesome standard English sleeps:
The varied and ample land, the North and South in the light,
and the voices of Earth and Moon swell in my helmet

with prarie inflections, soft twangs of outer speech—
"You're looking real good," says Earth.
"—ain't that somethin?"
"Roger. No sweat. Out."

Alternate Lives

Tired of trying to become
a morning of study a snowy morning of study
as if snow papered lips and hair
and lightened the myriad numbers and genders
(*but there is a fish as dark as me a bird*)
and all my papery profiles glowed and lightened

but the alternate lives call each on one clear tone
and the mind drifts backward like a paper boat
fragrant as this morning's treetrunks—
"Night Watchman Wanted." "Furnished Room to Rent"
then sailing on through the wall it leaves you
in the interior miles from human   you gave

news laws to the trees in tears these are my people
rough face streaming knotholes centennial rings
last glimpsed towards twilight by a rare
traveller to that brown north land—where an oar
is a winnowing fan the moon a handful of feathers—
a tiny trousered shape across the fathoms of distance

and still the alternative lives descend
depthless and evenhanded   still the line
of lighteyed bearded old women reappears
these lives honed down to three or four obsessions
these armchairs and grey arms that stream
slow television light . . .

even language grew too young to follow
nights alone in the tiny rented room
with the Polestar at the window   too huge   too white
dreaming still emptier rooms to dream
of rooms in—but at the far end
you saw the life those ancient lives projected

all your old neighborhoods are pasted over
with signs and arrows pointing to this hour
still you are not quite these not quite one breath
with the pleasant room the littered workdesk
that is for the snowstorm looking in
it knows what the good life is   so once did you.

JULIA RANDALL

Letter

The heat is terrific. The storms are terrible.
I have revised the tool closet. They are coming along
on the Science Building. They do not light
the altar at night. They have littered the lawn
with prunings from the elm.

It will not change here.
The mountains are one face.
A peasant said she'd watched the mountains grow
for thirty years. I know that is not true,
even without the texts. It is slow, slow,
earth's crust, rising and falling. The lavender
wild bergamot is in bloom, and the big-root
morning glory that furls up at night.
I have watched it, like I watched the cereus,
once, in an elegant parlor, bloom in an hour.
You cannot see them move, but they must.
It is like breathing. It is made clear in the text:
ripening, rottening. The proprietor
of the elegant parlor, a sixty-year-old widower,
made lead soldiers for a hobby, especially
historic grenadiers, dragoons and lancers.

I have cut my hair again. I have put up
the family photographs. Mother said
no one would know who that that girl — herself — was.

Have you found a new face
in your foreign desert?
Is space a constant mirror, and is time
its constant image, or vice versa?
You left the light on in the basement.
Your empty parking-slot and unkempt yard
image you like a mold. I can fill them in
with the old features. I do not feel love loosening.
Do forms harden in time?
It is not made clear in the text.
Do mountains grow?
Sometimes I think we are all illiterate,
breathing like lilies; spread so, furl so.

Loving I

I went a journey round the world of my body,
hitherto unexplored except in theory
conned in the class of Professor Ptolemy.

He mapped me well, knew where my sun was,
told me which routes to take, like Rand McNally
told me how to get to Indianapolis,
but couldn't describe the look of the place.

So I knew you were there. And I spelunked in the caves
and slippery passages, often on my knees,
tapping with my bonestaff, or climbing,
sometimes, on gray wires,

or lanterning, or calling, till I reached my skin
and sweated across it. But the sun
was farther, farther, forever not to be had.
It was then, I think, I called the cartographers bad.

Do not take the inland route, is my advice.
There are incomparable views of ice,
and jungle ambuscades still to be feared
on the southern roads, where the natives have not been cleared
out. I would say: Sail, sail
beyond the Islands of Spice, with the sun west,
the sun always other, the sun in an outer space.
How can we map what moves us? How can we tell
the risks of scouting?
If we fail, we fail.

Dream 2

And how or why they came, or who they were,
or who I was that met them, riding so
elated on the dream's crest, walking
in a real field, but without feeling
pebble or hummock grass, or the nerve leading
breast or thigh to beating; it was all
watery and shining. When they loosed
their arrows, it was finches
driven on the wind, long leaves, or schools of fishes
that darted through me, fell around and beyond
without a prick or sound. I remember them laughing,
so simple it was. And I remember them smiling.

Science and Poetry: Three Comments

1.

To grate the greenness of the green
Is not, mynheer, to desecrate
The grail of crusted artistry
Whose fictive emeralds wink as bright.

We two set forth from Camelot:
The analytic with his board
To bare the essential animal,
And you, my unaccoutred bard,
Describing sounds of hoo and ha,
And jigging at resemblances.

Our strategies, mynheer, diverge,
But Joseph keeps the chapel warm,
And curious questers up and down
Spy out the samite mysteries.

Record, doktor. And fool, jig on.

2.

The moon that was our mystery
Is that pocked orb and weary ash.

But who, careening in borrowed light,
Questions the cinder's potency?

As if the new geography
Were parenthetic to our scheme—

As if, occasionally, one caught
Echoes of actual Artemis.

3.

There is no limiting of the blue
That leaps above the blue beyond.
There is the unwillingness to look
Over the frosty burdock's head
In this December floor of light.

In this December floor of light
As if the shimmering twig were all,
And dull that pierceless cupola.

So dull that pierceless cupola,
Imagination flaked beneath:
As if the gods themselves were cast
In moods of ours to icy death.

Kinderscenen

1

Sometimes I live alone.
I am a stone.
I cannot hear the wind
for I am blind.
I cannot taste the leaf
for I am deaf.
I cannot touch the sun.
I am a stone.

2

My legs are two winds,
my arms are two other.
Who is my father?
Who is my mother?
Where do they send me?
When will they call?
Look over the mountain,
look under the stall,
rattle the rooftree,
flatten the hay,
Four winds, will you never
rest from play?

3

I am soft as the sea,
I am long as a river,
small as the rain
that sings forever.

I am diamond as dew,
I am shapes of snow.
Wherever the seasons go,
I go.

4

Sometimes I live in the moon.
Far, not soon.
Near, not late.
And white, white.

The Bennett Springs Road

I knew it was there, if I'd had time to look:
the sweet water falling over rock,
the leaf-mold floor, secret to all but light,
the tall boles stationed between day and night.

There is the heart of the mountain, not the crest.
Season and century league in some high place,
impulsive powers that beat the peak to sand
and scatter Appalachian on the wind.

And lie at last by the little stream that brings
all gods to truth. On the road to Bennett Springs,
tired of the paltry ridges, I lay down
the last of my youth where all the gods had grown,
became the water falling over the stone,
became the forest-father to red men,
became the tribe of stars, both daughter and son,
the mother of moss, the bird that sang I am.

Notes from the Poets

ALAN WILLIAMSON: When I was a child my parents lived in Chicago, but all of our relatives lived in California, and so we drove across the country and back every summer. Partly because of these trips I have a liking for the expanses of America, for travel and restlessness, that somewhat takes the place of the exclusive attachment some people feel for one single place. Virginia brings this restlessness home to me because, though I like it, my being here is entirely an accident of the teaching profession—it is as if I had arbitrarily stayed behind in any of the appealing small towns my family drove through. Some of this gets in "Spring Trains" I think. "A Progress of the Soul" uses California settings—and details about my European ancestors—but its landscapes are basically metaphorical: a child's sense of being fixed in a formidably preexisting world, as against as adolescent's imaginative ability to go far off inside and take the world along with him.

AMANDA BULLINS: An old person I met through my job has excellent vision and says the secret is looking alternately at the distant mountains and print close at hand. I have not mastered this focusing exercise, but I often look at the horizon in early evening when there is a blue-green rim of light that separates the dark mountain shapes from the dark sky. I am in this place, the Roanoke Valley, that is both protected and also full of held-in pollution. I have experienced some difficulty in judging physical distance and spatial relationships, and this may have influenced me to describe people in terms of where they are or where they have been. The trouble with trying to be a writer and live in this valley is that one could easily spend hours standing like an okra pod in a garden and more hours searching Bent Mountain for a wanted house with land, me with my sheep/dog terrier and my $2.00 table-top Christmas cedar and my Bookla Bear (sweetie, honey) across town with no dog but an eight-foot pine, meeting and drawing apart, living the contrasts, not writing about them.

JOSEPH GARRISON: I live between two mountain ranges—Blue Ridge and Allegheny—and their forests, draws, and fire towers hold my attention. I take my bearings in the wind, facing south. I like clear days, particularly in the dry seasons. I pray for rain and worry about floods. I think about birthdays, burials, and buildings. I open the doors of my house and ask people in. Some do, and some don't, enter. I think about that, too. I try to write poems. They come very slowly. I wait, sometimes too long. Maybe the land cultivates retinal and mental patience. And maybe patience has something to do with distance. I think that would be true for me.

RUDY SHACKELFORD: If the concepts "landscape" and "distance" have any relation at all to my work, it is rather to that aural space where the music of verse reverberates than to any topographical transposition from the landscape of Virginia (of America, of the Western Hemisphere, of the Universe!) to which they refer. My own work is athematic. If someone wished to do so, I would countenance the substitution of my "meaningful" English words for a nonsense language having precisely equivalent qualities of weight, texture, color, and so on. That is to say, the logic of my poetry is that of assonance, alliteration, tone, rime, meter, and cadence—not of ideas or conceptualized feelings. On the other hand, nothing would be more foreign to, or destructive of, my work than translating it into another standard language and superimposing thereby a totally alien network of aural values. Each language is the matrix of a literature quarried from it by native laborers for whom "landscape and distance", aural and visual, are modes of sensory apprehension irreplaceable and uninterchangeable because indelibly imprinted upon the central nervous system.

RICHARD McCANN: I came to Richmond, Virginia, when I was seventeen of my own free will. After being raised in the suburbs of Washington, D.C., it was as if I'd gotten off in the first port whose language and traditions were foreign to me. Though I've traveled away since, often for months at a time, I return to Virginia now because it is familiar to me. That is, it is familiar in the way a landscape is familiar in a dream, familiar through studying it a long time. I am writing this while riding in the Dome Car of a train across Wyoming, and outside the landscape stretches so bare and planetary I don't know how to see it. I'm distracted by the voices up ahead of a couple from Bristol describing Virginia to an Alaskan. They rattle off the employment rates, the population, regional products, average income. While I consider myself above all a traveler in not only the metaphorical sense but, more importantly, the *literal* one, my impulse is to leave off looking at this prairie and help them describe our home.

My feeling for landscape might be best explained through a description. I remember driving alone for hours through the dark southwestern mountains, only, after a sharp turn, to arrive at a new K-Mart. At least a hundred people were lined up along the road in their trucks and cars, watching the parking lot, their headlights on. Inside, someone told me, the police were hunting down a burglar in the aisles. When they finally shot him, the store lights came on and for an instant we saw him stand, then fall behind a huge banner that read, "Dollar Daze." It's hard to figure how the mountains fit into this story, but they do. We started up our cars and drove home. My interest in landscape is in how it makes people live—be it laundromat, mountain or swamp—and for a moment in this landscape the K- Mart was more real than anything and the landscape was, as Adrienne Rich puts it, "condemned scenery."

MARGARET GIBSON: The words *landscape* and *distance* suggest to me two other words, *vision* and *memory*. I have always looked at the land and remember particularly certain fields, weeds, rivers in Amelia and Gloucester counties. There is distance, of course, implied in vision, for we cannot see what is up too close. And there is distance in memory which, while bringing us closer to the unlost past, also whispers that much else has vanished or that what we now remember has taken a new construction. Admittedly, these nice distinctions don't matter much, except in paragraphs like this. They don't intrude consciously in writing poems. And they certainly don't matter when you work the land rather than look at it, as I discovered keeping a garden the size of a small farm whose soil was more suited to pottery than to plants. You don't *look* at the lovely things grow—you get in there with them.

But primarily I want to talk about distance. Perhaps some think it a bad word. But I am thinking of distance as a good word, as the necessary space between myself and the other which makes perception possible, and as the necessary solitude which makes possible a steadiness and a capacity for faith in oneself which, in turn, lets an ability to love others openly grow. "No one can become the shape of his thought, yet everyone tries," says a character in a novel I'm fond of. He's saying what distance is all about. The shape of the land, of the poem, of the garden, of the self—the shapes may be ideal or remembered, but they *change*. They are the possibilities we grow toward, coming closer as we go, taking them in.

PETER FELLOWES: To a young man raised among the tidy neighborhoods, square blocks and tabletop landscapes of a Chicago suburb, the Virginia countryside was an exotic excursion into a zone of the natural world which seemed, by contrast, almost tropical. Before Virginia, nature was a place you visited—an arboretum, a greenhouse, the narrow rectangle of my mother's flower garden—or paged through in the gorgeous color plates of a Christmas gift book. On a family vacation, it was nice in the back seat to imagine actually living in a cabin among the hills and rivers and forestland outside the window. And so, when I first came to Virginia, it was enough just to sit on the floor of the pine forest behind my house and wonder down the deep ravine beneath me at the waxy bushes of rhododendron, the upstart cedar trees and the enormous spread of a lone beach tree, none of which had ever sat in the wheelbarrow of a nursery man. Now I can stand in the lacy shade of our grove of honey locusts and watch the oriole light on the bending milkweed in the pasture, I can feel the chill on my bare forearms the instant the sun has fallen behind our mountain, and I look around and know that I am at home. I admire the conscientiousness of natural things, turning humbly toward the sun and being—their sweet spiritual health. I feel we share this silence, this alternation of light and darkness, this submission to death.

DABNEY STUART: With the exception of five academic seasons (the source of whose calendrical shape, it pleases me to remember, is agricultural), three summers in Boston and the Berkshires, and one gelid, debilitating gestation near the northern border of our country, I have lived in Virginia. This was at first accidental, then inescapable, and for the last eight years or so has become a matter of choice. Many areas would, I suspect, provide the temperate climate and mountainous terrain I prefer, and I could probably find in other regions stages compatible with my progress *ex urbe*; Virginia is particular, however, because it nurtures my past, and certain parts of it have become familiar enough to be mysterious. It takes years, decades, to learn to be in a place (these five words almost need to be hyphenated) and I do not think I could begin that development again, even if I wished to. And, odd as it sounds, there are many lives— transparent, remote—I act as agent for who would grieve my leaving.

JAMES EVERHARD: All landscapes are essentially alien landscapes. I bring them into myself by looking at them, but I am never a part of them because they are always out there. There is always some kind of tension between me and the landscape like the tension of water that keeps it from being outside of itself. I can only be in someone else's landscape and someone else can be in mine. That's what is important about landscape. I, can look at a landscape when no one is there and still see someone because I once saw someone there or in a similar landscape. Human landscapes are always very close at hand because they are filled with objects that obstruct the view. The farther I can see into landscape the more alien, the more empty it must be. I bring all sorts of deceits to the landscape. The mind and the eye see different things. But ultimately only the landscape, as it is, is there. I rarely look at a landscape, then, but am always looking at something else. I may think the landscape is helping me to see what is inside me but what is inside me is actually only feelings. Men dream uncautiously against the grain of things. What I want to be in the landscape is not there; hence tension. No landscape is home. We are all nomads, passing through. Nothing out there is ours inside. We leave nothing behind. However we try to shape what is out there, it will not be shaped. It has its own shape.

KATE JENNINGS: It seems there's a certain point in adolescence when a person chooses, or claims, his country, so to speak, a landscape of the heart that will be his, and his home, all his life. Mine was Richmond, and what a sad dumpy city in the late fifties! My family moved there from Louisville, and we felt we'd entered a true wasteland. But I loved Richmond then, in spite of itself, and came to feel a defensive pride in it, and amusement at its eccentricities, and fond chagrin at its provincialism. I felt I was engaged in a bittersweet war: the people I wanted to write to, for, about, were the very ones who wouldn't read me, literally or figuratively. Poetry was something ladies did, like joining a garden club.

Later I went to school in southwest Virginia, at Emory and Henry College, near the Tennessee border, and again I encountered that frustrating stubbornness, that refusal to risk anything new or strange, that *suspicion of change*. Among mountains whose sheer beauty would knock you to your knees, these people were concerned with such issues as women smoking cigarettes, or wearing pants (except between the hours of two and four on Saturday afternoons). *Dance* was a dirty word, so we went to fraternity parties where we *functioned.* Two by two.

I fought it and loved it and scorned it and finally left it for Chicago, intending to finish school there. But I was more haunted and caught than I knew, and a year later I was back. My husband was teaching at Emory when I met him, and when we moved to New York the next year, we both felt we were going into exile.

DAVID JEDDIE SMITH: A Negro porter in William Styron's *Lie Down in Darkness* says of the Tidewater area of Virginia, which is my home, that it is a "poontang town, sho enough." It is a galaxy of implications, including fecundity, joy, heat, night brawling, sea breezes, plain men and women who live on the nubs of their nerves. I have known since before I started to write that the world I have always regarded as symbolic of a larger existence moved right there around me, from Yorktown to Pungo. Tidewater is not a poontang town any longer. It is shopping malls and military bases and Little League diamonds. But bottomless hulks in the marshes and weathered shacks of the fishermen still suggest the value of living one's life with honor and grace. They provide the images and the nourishment for whatever permanence and wisdom I am able to weave into my poems. Though I reside hundreds of miles inland, I live with the swamps and tides and derelicts.

GARY SANGE: What happens when space is unconsciously comprehended all day? Where does that space go when I dream? Is there a prairie circling in my brain? Or to put it other ways, I live on a farm. Wait all year for the rippling blue-green barley field before my eye to stretch out into the teeth of a slow combine harvesting all the way to the plum-colored tobacco barn against the sky. When the long ravine of harvested barley arrives, the barn itself appears to be tunneled out. I can see how its side doors had been swung open and covered up the whole time the barley was tall. How the revealed open barn is now a plum-colored boxcar waiting. From this threshhold of new distance, the horizon pulls back to let in a view of rippling, blue-green river on the other side. I will never catch up with the vanishing through that frame of sky.

I hope the barn-boxcar is inevitably come upon and not just a trick of diction. I've had to ask what happens to space because everywhere I look I begin a distance that later arrives. I am constantly overtaken by, and constantly catching up with, where I am. That is not as exasperatingly paradoxical as it sounds: I perceive by following out the motion implicit in shape. In a poem of mine, "Long after the Accident," the speaker gazes at a fender about which he says, "impact, in a coma of momentum, ripples through wrinkled steel." And the lighthouse keeper in the poem included here must "keep his eye out for something irregular on the waves." Chase the vectors:

that's kept me going. And so has Ted Roethke, who says: "We recover tenderness by long looking."

QUENTIN VEST: What is universal in poetry must have its origin in what is hopelessly private. For example, I can make my poem "Serein" more public by explaining its strange title and how I chose it, but I cannot explain what the landscape and the weather of that poem mean to me, or how I crossed the distance from a certain kind of weather to the idea of a thing to be made, a poem to be written. Keats breathed the "pure serene" of Homer's landscape when he heard Chapman's translation. The word *serene* comes from the French *serein* and is actually a meterological term which means "a fine rain falling from a cloudless sky shortly after sunset." The English word would not permit me to count on the literal sense of *the serene* or *serein*, so important to the landscape of my poem. For *serein* is two weathers at once, two states of being, thus two landscapes, the important one seen through the eyes of the lost other, undefiled by the distance from which I am there.

BRUCE GUERNSEY: I have lived in Virginia now for seven years, mostly in the Tidewater region. My early poems were very much influenced by living in and around these historical areas as I tried to capture some of the ironic parallels and differences in our history then and the problems of the sixties—from 1969 on, when I started writing. As can be seen from my poem here, I haven't completely abandoned some of these concerns, only, I feel, learned to handle them better. And the landscapes are more internal—the houses of the poems, I'm told by friends, are psychological states. So I've become more withdrawn, have followed Roethke's black bird "deep in the brain, far back," have moved, I guess, from United States to psychological ones.

JOHN ALEXANDER ALLEN: I read somewhere that the landscapes of one's poems are always that of childhood. This is true of my poems, apparently, where water predominates—the sea and woodsy ponds—and islands rather than mountains turn up again and again. The mountains of Virginia provide a splendid setting for rumination—I am looking at one of them through my study window as I write. However, in my imagination these settings that are not nautical are likely to be strictly urban: city streets, department stores, labyrinthine hotels. Or they are nowheres of no particular topographical interest. I dreamed that I was crossing a frontier into the land of "femenye." For a moment I had the lost feeling of a foreigner in a strange and possibly threatening land. Then, without words, I was given to understand that I was a native of this country also—one without mountains, ponds or seashore. I feel very much at home in Virginia and am, I hope, grateful for the beauties which surround me here in the hills. But I must leave them to another poet to celebrate as they deserve. In writing poems, I work largely from the inside out and must be content with any country that dreams choose to place me in.

HENRY TAYLOR: "Landscape" and "distance" seem to me to contradict each other. Though I have lived in the West, and have seen landscapes more than a day's walk away, I grew up on Loudoun County, where whatever I saw at any one time seemed to be within reach. In those days I thought concretely about what I saw; I would wonder whether I could get to a certian place on horseback, and whether the farming there would require my going around, or permit my going through. And I was interested in anecdotes and historical facts about various pieces of land. All these attitudes are fairly traditional among rural southerners, I suppose; and I suppose that most of my values would be traditionally southern, were it not for my Quaker heritage, which has sometimes been significantly at odds with the values and attitudes that shaped much of the rural South. The tensions inherent in being a southern Quaker are evident, to me at least, in the best of my poems. For example, I simultaneously love and distrust tradition, ceremony, form; I value the humorous elements that turn up in the gravest of circumstances; and, though I dislike most kinds of change, I have an almost affectionate toleration for the fact of death.

ANNIE DILLARD: I've scarcely been anywhere *but* Virginia. Virginia is all I know, and therefore everything to me. If you stay put long enough in one place, without doing anything, you're bound to learn something.

ANNE WINTERS: I take landscape first for the world of everything we see. Every moment that our eye is open, distance is leading it from the near part of that world, with its detailed and particular figures, to a realm of hazier, more generally perceived forms; beyond these lies the unseen. This physical experience of vision, so intimate and daily, is in a way symmetrical with our sense of inner landscape. Immediately behind our eyes seem to lie the perceptions and responses of our immediate, perceptible personality. "Behind" this, so to speak, is the less conscious area where particularities and individuals are blurred, where responses are overwhelming but unclear—the world of primary human responses; beyond this, all consciousness is extinguished in the purely material processes of the body. In day-to-day life we experience the distinctness and harmony of these two symmetrical, mutually sonorous landscapes as poising on the membrane of attention and of perception.

But in landscape I am fascinated by the rear-ground, the distance into which the perspective lines are always receding. If we lived in the indistinct zone of vision instead of in its foreground, we would live in improverishment of particular attention and expectation. We would always be prepared to collide with ideal and millenarian forms, for we would be on the very edge of the vanishing point, which, in both worlds, is the extinction of perception itself.

JULIA RANDALL: I do not think lyric poets are "after" anything; when they are, they're suspect. Or say one is simply "after" one's sense of things, which making poetry reveals or, of course making art of any sort. Imagery derives from temperament and circumstance; forms and concerns from cultural history. I don't expect Wordsworth set out to write about Nature, nor indeed is that his real subject, though he might have said so. In fact, he writes about epistemology, psychology, and the natural conditions of faith. So there. In short, there is the subject—a rainy day, etc.—and there is the Subject. One is, finally, interested in the human mind and its strange powers. It is something about these powers that is revealed, quite *im*personally.

Yes, living in Virginia "influenced" me: landscape, place names. Vermont and Maryland and Wyoming would do as well—only for me not the city and not foreign soil. I can't possibly *explain* that. I am rooted in robins and deciduous trees and English Language. But not by design. It all sounds so fatuous. However, the imagination is fascinating and the world is much in need of it. I get sick hearing about the *real*. Nothing is realer than the—er—spirit. Nothing is less real than Watergate and the energy crisis. Relations are real, as Uncle Henry reminds us. Values are real, as Uncle Matthew reminds us. Perception is real, as William Wordsworth reminds us. And we are real, as poetry reminds us.